Mother, I Love You

Written by Roy Honegger
Cover Design and Typography by Roy Honegger and
Dmitry Feygin

Published by Great Quotations Publishing Co.,
Glendale Heights, IL

Library of Congress Catalog Card Number: 97-078978

ISBN 1-56245-278-9

Printed in Hong Kong

When I stopped seeing my mother with the eyes of a child,
I saw the woman who helped me give birth to myself.

—*Nancy Friday*

The mother is the most precious possession of the nation, so precious that society advances its highest well-being when it protects the functions of the mother.

—Ellen Key

A mother is neither cocky, nor proud, because she knows the school principal may call at any minute to report that her child had just driven a motorcycle through the gymnasium.

—*Mary Kay Blakely*

Life is the first gift,
love the second and
understanding the third.

—*Marge Piercy*

A mother's love is like an island.
In life's ocean vast and wide, a peaceful,
quiet shelter from the restless, rising tide.

—Helen Steiner Rice

7

I have three great children.
I realize how fast childhood goes,
so I cherish it that much more.

—*Sally Field*

The little things that I never really noticed all come back now as I have my own daughter. Thanks, Mom, for being such a strong model for me. You made it seem easy.

—*Meredith Ralston*

God knows that a mother needs fortitude and courage and tolerance and flexibility and patience and firmness and nearly every other brave aspect of the human soul.

—Phyllis McGinley

In the sheltered simplicity of the first days after a baby is born, one sees again the magical closed circle, the miraculous sense of two people existing only for each other.

—Anne Morrow Lindbergh

Mommy herself has told us that she looked upon us more as her friends than her daughters. Now that is all very fine, but still, a friend can't take a mother's place. I need my mother as an example which I can follow. I want to be able to respect her.

—Anne Frank

Your children are always your "babies",
even if they have gray hair.

—Janet Leigh

Mom is a tough friend.
I know she is going to be honest with me.

—Robert Eldridge

Mothers have to handle all kinds of situations.
When presented with the new baby brother he said he wanted,
the toddler told his mother, "I changed my mind."

—Judith Viorst

My mother is drawn to need and the sweetness of the needy.
My warmest memories of my mother are from times when
I was sick, or in pain, or in some kind of trouble.

—Susan Cheever

I looked at this tiny, perfect creature and it was as though a light switch had been turned on. A great rush of love, mother love, flooded out of me.

—Madeleine L'Engle

Being a mother makes me feel as if
I got my membership in an exclusive club.

—Andie MacDowell

I've gained a great feeling of peace from being a mother…
The ability to love is the heart of the matter.

—Gloria Vanderbilt

A mother is not a person to lean on but
a person to make leaning unnecessary.

— *Dorothy Canfield Fisher*

It goes without saying that you should never have
more children than you have car windows.

—*Erma Bombeck*

A babe at the breast is as much pleasure
as the bearing is pain.

—*Marion Zimmer Bradley*

A mother's love is an ocean; a vast and powerful force which reaches unspeakable depths.

—*Roderick Van Murchison*

I've always felt I've had luck, certainly in obvious areas.
And now I have the greatest blessing of all—these children.

—Jessica Lange

What would I want on my gravestone for posterity? "Mother."

—*Jessica Lange*

It's the little things you do day in and day out that count.
That's the way you teach your children.

—*Amanda Pays*

Thou art thy mother's glass, and she in thee
Calls back the lovely April of her prime.

—*William Shakespeare*

Our first mother-daughter outing: For three hours, knitting our thoughts and lives together like old college roommates going toward a reunion.

—Phyllis Theroux

And she spake out with a loud voice, and said, "Blessed art thou among women, and blessed is the fruit of thy womb."

—Luke 1:42, KJV

What feeling is so nice as a child's hand in yours?
So small, so soft and warm, like a kitten huddling
in the shelter of your clasp.

—Marjorie Holmes

The love I feel for my child is like a balloon that keeps filling up and expanding. It never bursts; it just keeps getting bigger and bigger. Maybe, over a lifetime, the love will fill many balloons!

—Judy Schmidt

The great high of winning Wimbledon lasts for about a week…
But having a baby—there just isn't any comparison.

—Chris Evert

Some are kissing mothers and some are scolding mothers, but it is love just the same, and most mothers kiss and scold together.

—*Pearl S. Buck*

I love being a mother. I am more aware. I feel things on a deeper level. I seem to have more of everything now: more love, more magic, more energy.

—*Shelley Long*

Women, who are, beyond all doubt, the mothers of all mischief, also nurse that babe to sleep when he is too noisy.

—*R. D. Blackmore*

So for the mother's sake, the child was dear,
And dearer was the mother for the child.

—*Samuel Taylor Coleridge*

A mother is she who can take the place of all others
but whose place no one else can take.

—*Cardinal Mermillod*

Mother's arms are made of tenderness,
and sweet sleep blesses the child who lies therein.

—*Victor Hugo*

There is no influence so powerful as that of the mother.

—Sarah Josepha Hale

When there is a mother in the house,
matters speed well.

—*Amos Bronson Alcott*

The God to whom little boys say their prayers has a face
very much like their mother's.

—Sir James M. Barrie

Youth fades; love droops, the leaves of friendship fall;
A mother's secret hope outlives them all.

—*Oliver Wendell Holmes*

That best academy, a mother's knee.

—*James Russell Lowell*

A mother's love perceives no impossibilities.

—Paddock

The angels…singing unto one another,
can find among their burning terms of love,
none so devotional as that of 'mother.'

—Edgar Allen Poe

Sometimes the poorest woman leaves
her children the richest inheritance.

—*Ruth E. Renkel*

Of all the rights of women, the greatest is to be a mother.

—Lin Yutang

There is no influence so powerful as that of the mother.

—*Sarah Josepha Hale*

In motherhood there's so much to learn, so much to give,
and although the learning gets less with each child,
the giving never does.

—Marguerite Kelly

Any mother could perform the jobs of
several air traffic controllers with ease.

—*Lisa Alther*

A mother's heart is a baby's most beautiful dwelling.

—*Ed Dussault*

A mother's love is patient and forgiving
when all others are forsaking,
and it never fails or falters even though
the heart is breaking.

—*Helen Steiner Rice*

My mother's love for me was so great that
I have worked hard to justify it.

—Marc Chagall

One mother achieves more than a hundred teachers.

—*Jewish Proverb*

My mother is a poem I'll never be able to write though everything I write is a poem to my mother.

—Sharon Doubiago

Be kind to thy mother, for when thou were young,
who loved thee so fondly as she?

—*Margaret Courtney*

Men are what their mothers made them.

—*Ralph Waldo Emerson*

It was my mother who taught us to stand up to our problems, not only in the world around us but in ourselves.

—Dorothy Pitman Hughes

Who ran to help me when I fell,
And would some pretty story tell,
Or kiss the place to make it well?
My mother.

—*Anne Taylor*

All that I am or hope to be, I owe to my mother.

— *Abraham Lincoln*

No matter how old a mother is, she watches her middle-aged children for signs of improvement.

—*Florida Scott-Maxwell*

There is no friendship, no love,
like that of the mother for her child.

—*Henry Ward Beecher*

Dear Mother–You know that nothing can ever change what we have always been and will always be to each other.

—*Franklin D. Roosevelt*

Give love to a little child, and you get a great deal back.

—John Ruskin

Mothers of daughters are daughters of mothers and have remained so, in circles joined to circles, since time began.

—Signe Hammer

In the woman's keeping is committed the destiny
of the generations to come after them.

—Theodore Roosevelt

And so our mothers and grandmothers have, more often
than not anonymously, handed on the creative spark,
the seed of the flower they themselves never hoped to see,
or like a sealed letter they could not plainly read.

—*Alice Walker*

A child without a mother is like a door without a doorknob.

—*Yiddish Proverb*

It's not flesh and blood, but the heart
that makes us mothers and daughters.

—Anonymous

My Mother:
She always tried to impress upon me the importance
of treating everybody as you want to be treated.

—*Albert Bethune*

A mother's patience is like a tube of toothpaste—
it's never quite gone.

—Anonymous

A good mother is like a quilt—she keeps her children warm
but doesn't smother them.

—Unknown

A woman is her mother.

—*Anne Sexton*

Mother: The person who sits up with you when you are sick, and puts up with you when you are well.

—*Anonymous*

It was when I had my first child that I understood
how much my mother loved me.

—Anonymous

Children are a great comfort in your old age. And they help you reach it sooner, too.

—*Lionel M. Kauffman*

There would have to be something wrong with someone who could throw out a child's first Valentine card saying, "I love you, Mommy."

—Ginger Hutton

We are now told that automation is a process that
gets all the work done while you just stand there.
When we were younger, this process was called MOTHER.

—Anonymous

Our mothers and grandmothers, some of them;
moving to music not yet written.

—Alice Walker

The woman who bore me is no longer alive but I seem to be her daughter in increasingly profound ways.

—*Johnetta B.Cole*

You can multiply all the relations of life, have more than one sister or brother; in the course of events, but you never can have but one mother!

—Anonymous

Mother to Daughter:
I long to put the experience of fifty years at once into your young lives, to give you at once the key of that treasure chamber every gem of which has cost me tears and struggles and prayers, but you must work for these inward treasures yourselves.

—Harriet Beecher Stowe

Motherhood is not for the fainthearted. Used frogs, skinned knees, and the insults of teenage girls are not meant for the wimpy.

—Danielle Steele

Most mothers are instinctive philosophers.

—*Harriet Beecher Stowe*

We cannot put mothering into a formula and come up with a person who has the special feeling for your child that you do.

—Dr. Sally E. Shaywitz

To My Mother
From where have you learned to wipe the tears,
To quietly bear the pain,
To hide in your heart the cry, the hurt
The suffering and the complaint?
From where is this quiet in your heart,
From where have you learned strength?

—*Hannah Senesh*

To describe my mother would be to write about
a hurricane in its perfect power.

—*Maya Angelou*

Who takes the child by the hand, takes the mother by the heart.

—*Danish Proverb*

Daughter to Mother:
Mother, I have worn your name like a shield. It has torn
but protected me all these years...

—*Lucille Clifton*

Sometimes in the mirror, I see my mother in myself.

—*Jean Anderson*

My mother taught me to walk proud and tall
'as if the world were mine.' I remember that line,
and I think it brought me some luck.

—*Sophia Loren*

Mother is the name for God in the lips and hearts of children.

—*William Makepeace Thackery*

Don't turn a small problem into a big problem;
say yes to your mother.

—Sally Berger

Blessed is the mother who treats her child as she would be treated, for her home shall be filled with happiness.

—Lenora Zearfoss

Mother knows best.

—*Edna Ferber*

95

In search of my mother's garden, I found my own.

—*Alice Walker*

The best gift a mother can give her child is the gift of herself.

—*Anonymous*

Mighty is the force of motherhood!
It transforms all things by its vital heart.

—*George Eliot*

Daughter to mother:
O my mother...I still hear something new
in your increasing love!

—*Nelly Sachs*

I cannot forget my mother. Though not as sturdy as others,
she is my bridge. When I needed to get across, she steadied
herself long enough for me to run across safely.

—Renita Weems

Sit in the seat of thy mother
And walk in thy mother's footsteps.

—Johann Gottfried von Herder

Mothers know the way to rear children to be just; they know a simple, merry, tender knack of tying sashes, fitting baby shoes and stringing pretty words that make no sense.

—*Aurora Leigh*

My mother is a person who speaks with her life
as much as with her tongue.

—*Kesaya E. Noda*

There is no such thing as a non-working mother.

—Hester Mundis

Maybe Mom is my alter ego and the woman
I'm able to be when I'm working.

—*Mary Tyler Moore*

A Mother Is:
A happy, warm, patient person who plays games with her
children joyously, teaches them constantly, and takes them
to the doctor, the dentist, the zoo, the park, swimming
and camping - sometimes all on the same day.

—Shirley Radl

A mother understands what a child does not say.

—*Yiddish Proverb*

My mother wanted me to be her wings, to fly as she never quite had the courage to do. I love her for that.

—Erica Jong

God could not be everywhere and therefore he made mothers.

—Jewish Proverb

Blaming mother is just a negative way of clinging to her still.

—*Nancy Friday*

Daughter to Mother:
I think my life began with waking up
and loving my mother's face.

—*Mirah in George Eliot's "Daniel Deronda"*

A mother is a person who, seeing there
are only four pieces of pie for five people,
promptly announces she never did care for pie.

—Tenneva Jordan

There must always be a struggle between a mother and a daughter, while one aims at power the other at independence.

—*Unknown*

It is always our mother who makes us feel that we
belong to the better sort.

—*John L. Spalding*

One is not born a woman—one becomes one.

—*Simone De Beauvoir*

Being a full-time mother is one of the highest salaried jobs
in my field, since the payment is pure love.

—*Mildred B. Vermont*

I never thought you should be rewarded for
the greatest privilege of life.

—Mary Roper Cohen,
Mother of the Year, 1958

Motherhood is a profession by itself,
just like school teaching and lecturing.

—Ida B. Wells

Mother to Daughter:
I am giving you the dark birds of the night yes,
they are mine, they are mine to give.

—*Michele Murray*

In the eyes of its mother every beetle is a gazelle.

—*Moroccan Proverb*

Daughter to Mother:
You are like an everlasting friendship.
You are like a secret almost too wonderful to keep.
You are like the beginning, end and everything in between.
You are like a very knowledgeable volume of encyclopedia.
You are like you and I love you.

—Laurel O. Hoye

121

One mother is worth more than one hundred school masters.

—Anonymous

If evolution really works, how come mothers
have only two hands?

—Ed Dussault

The father is the head of the house—
the mother is the heart of the house.

—Unknown

You never get over being a child,
long as you have a mother to go to.

—*Sarah Orne Jewett*

The warmest bed of all is Mother's.

—Yiddish Proverb

The imprint of the mother remains
forever on the life of the child.

—Anonymous

Don't let these parenting years get away from you.
Your contributions to your children and grandchildren
could rank as your greatest accomplishments in life.

—Dr. James Dobson

What a mother says to her children is not heard by the world,
but it will be heard by posterity.

—Anonymous

Naps are the glue that hold mothers together.

—Unknown

What is home without a mother?

—Alice Hawthorne

Mothers are and are not made.

—George Middleton

My little mother, my star, my courage, my own.

—*Katherine Mansfield*

My Mother:
She's my teacher, my adviser, my greatest inspiration.

—*Whitney Houston*

Mother is a word called Love.
And all the world is mindful of
the love that's given and shown to others
is different from the love of Mothers...

—*Helen Steiner Rice*

She's always seemed invincible to me.
She just kept going forward.

—Julie Nixon Eisenhower,
on her mother, Pat Nixon

Mothers are granted a single decade in which to lay a foundation of values and attitudes that will help their children cope with the future pressures and problems of adulthood.

—Dr. James Dobson

The mother is the medium which the primitive infant transforms himself into a socialized human being.

—*Beata Rank*

Don't give young people advice. Don't tell them about your ailments. And don't say, 'When I was a young girl...'

—*Sonia Zeger Hodes*

The quickest way to get your children's attention
is to sit down and look comfortable.

—*Unknown*

The very essence of motherly love is to care for the child's growth, and that means to want the child's separation from herself.

—*Erich Fromm*

Mother:
She never outgrows the burden of love, and to the end
she carries the weight of hope for those she bore.

—Florida Scott-Maxwell

When God thought of MOTHER, He must have laughed with satisfaction, and framed it quickly, so rich, so deep, so divine, so full of soul, power, and beauty, was the conception.

—Henry Ward Beecher

The future of society is in the hands of mothers.

—De Beaufort

And it came to me, and I knew what I had to have before my soul would rest. I wanted to belong, to belong to my mother. And in return, I wanted my mother to belong to me.

—Gloria Vanderbilt

To my first Love, my Mother, on whose knee I learnt love—
love that is not troublesome.

—*Christina Rossetti*

What do you do with mother love and mother wit
when the babies are grown and gone away?

—*Joanne Greenberg*

The mother loves her child most divinely, not when she surrounds him with comfort and anticipates his wants, but when she resolutely holds him to the highest standards and is content with nothing less than his best.

—Hamilton Wright Mabie

We bear the world, and we make it… There was never a great man who had not a great mother—it is hardly an exaggeration.

—*Olive Schreiner*

The mother's heart is the child's schoolroom.

—*Henry Ward Beecher*

Portrait of Mother:
She was the light and not the lamp.

—*Jessamyn West*

Children are the anchors that hold a mother to life.

—*Sophocles*

Nothing else will ever make you as happy or as sad,
as proud or as tired, as motherhood.

—Elia Parsons

Truth, which is important to a scholar, has got to be concrete.
And there's nothing more concrete than dealing
with babies, burps, bottles and frogs.

—*Jeanne Kirkpatrick*

A family is a unit composed not only of children, but of fathers, mothers, an occasional animal and at times, the common cold.

—Ogden Nash

A mother is…
a parent who remains sane only because she never knows
what her three-year-old is going to do next.

—*Evan Esar*

When we see great men and women,
we give credit to their mothers.

—*Charlotte Perkins Gilman*

Other things may change us,
but we start and end with the family.

—*Anthony Brandt*

Mothers are the most unselfish,
the most responsible people in the world.

—Bernard M. Baruch

There is only one pretty child in the world,
and every mother has it.

—*English Proverb*

A child's hand in ycurs—what tenderness and power it arouses. You are instantly the very touchstone of wisdom and strength.

—Marjorie Holms

My mother had a great deal of trouble with me,
but I think she enjoyed it.

—*Mark Twain*

A man loves his sweetheart the most, his wife the best,
but his mother the longest.

—*Irish Proverb*

The joys of mothers and fathers are secret,
and so are their griefs and fears.

—Francis Bacon

We never know the love of the parent until
we become parents ourselves.

—Henry Ward Beecher

Being a mother, as far as I can tell, is a constantly evolving process of adapting to the needs of your child while also changing and growing as a person in your own right.

—*Deborah Insel*

If motherhood is an occupation which is critically important
to society the way we say it is, then there should be
a mother's bill of rights.

—*Barbara Ann Mikulski*

Other Titles By Great Quotations

201 Best Things Ever Said
The ABC's of Parenting
As a Cat Thinketh
The Best of Friends
The Birthday Astrologer
Chicken Soup & Other Yiddish Say
Cornerstones of Success
Don't Deliberate ... Litigate!
Fantastic Father, Dependable Dad
Global Wisdom
Golden Years, Golden Words
Grandma, I Love You
Growing up in Toyland
Happiness is Found Along The Way
Hollywords
Hooked on Golf
In Celebration of Women
Inspirations Compelling Food for Thought
I'm Not Over the Hill
Let's Talk Decorating
Life's Lessons
Life's Simple Pleasures
A Light Heart Lives Long
Money for Nothing, Tips for Free

Mother, I Love You
Motivating Quotes for Motivated People
Mrs. Aesop's Fables
Mrs. Murphy's Laws
Mrs. Webster's Dictionary
My Daughter, My Special Friend
Other Species
Parenting 101
Reflections
Romantic Rhapsody
The Secret Language of Men
The Secret Language of Women
Some Things Never Change
The Sports Page
Sports Widow
Stress or Sanity
Teacher is Better than Two Books
Teenage of Insanity
Thanks from the Heart
Things You'll Learn if You Live Long Enough
Wedding Wonders
Working Women's World
Interior Design for Idiots
Dear Mr. President

GREAT QUOTATIONS PUBLISHING COMPANY
1967 Quincy Court
Glendale Heights, IL 60139 - 2045
Phone (630) 582-2800
Fax (630) 582- 2813